Wakefield
Words

Wakefield Words

Richard Bell

based on

*A List of Provincial Words in use at Wakefield
in Yorkshire 1865*

collected by

William Stott Banks

Willow Island Editions

Also by Richard Bell
Walks in the Rhubarb Triangle
Walks in Robin Hood's Yorkshire
All Sorts of Walks in Liquorice Country
Walks around Ossett
Walks around Horbury
Walks around Newmillerdam
Around Old Horbury
Around Old Ossett
Thornes Park
Waterton's Park
Sandal Castle
Yorkshire Rock

Willow Island Editions
41 Water Lane, Middlestown,
Wakefield, WF4 4Px
www.willowisland.co.uk

ISBN 978-1-902467-22-1

Based on
A List of Provincial Words in use at Wakefield in Yorkshire
Collected by William Stott Banks
of Wakefield
(London: J. Russell Smith, Soho Square
Wakefield: W. R. Hall, Kirkgate)
1865

Contents

Ahhtwood
OUTWOOD

Ollathorp
ALVERTHORPE

Boggard of
Langar hede

Flansil
Laane
FLANSHAW
LANE

Hahse
o'Krekshon
PRISON

Goodybahr
GOODY BOWER

Weskit
Common
WESTGATE
COMMON

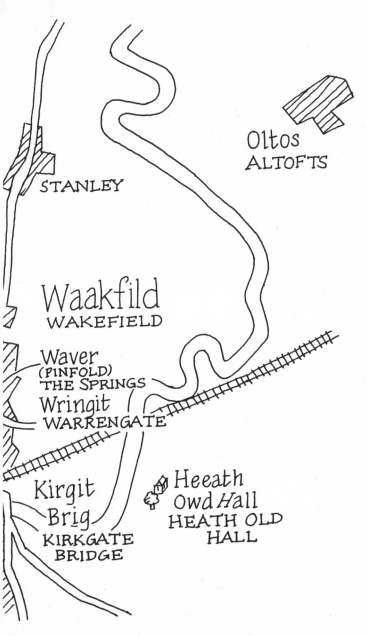

Oltos
ALTOFTS

STANLEY

Waakfild
WAKEFIELD

Waver
(PINFOLD)
THE SPRINGS

Wringit
WARRENGATE

Kirgit
Brig
KIRKGATE
BRIDGE

Heeath
Owd *Hall*
HEATH OLD
HALL

7

WILLIAM STOTT BANKS

Author's Address

W. S. Banks Esq
Solicitor
Northgate
Wakefield

Introduction

WHAT WOULD it be like if we could step back in time and see Wakefield as it was? What would we have heard people saying? What kind of food did they eat?

Old documents, photographs and prints don't tell the full story and the small, every-day details of our lives often get left out of history, so we're lucky that in 1865, Wakefield solicitor **William Stott Banks** (1820-1872) took the trouble to collect some of the words and phrases that he'd heard around town.

His sample sentences give us brief glimpses of street life;

> "Shoo dipt t' brush into t'gutter *h*oil an slahted *h*im all ower wi mucky watter"

But mid-Victorian Wakefield wasn't all mean streets and dark satanic mills; rural phrases like "T' litter o' pigs cam skutterin aht o' t' coit" and "larpin' ketlocks" [weeding charlock] remind us that fields and pastures were never very far away.

My thanks to Richard Knowles of the Rickaro Bookshop, Horbury, for bringing Banks' book, *Provincial Words in use at Wakefield*, to my attention.

PREFACE

From Banks' 'Provincial Words', 1865

THIS BOOK which contains such "provincial" words, now or lately in use at Wakefield, as I can call to mind or hear of, is printed as a step toward something better.

The list is not put forth as complete, for there must be local words which it does not contain; nor as including only expressions specially belonging to this town or district, because no place can have more than a few peculiarities, and whatever be the origin of a word it is almost sure to be employed in several neighboring dialects. Therefore, natives of Barnsley, Ossett, Batley, Leeds, or Bradford, may find many of their sayings in use amongst us, slightly differing in sound; but people from Whitby, or from Staiths or other parts of Cleveland, or from, Muker or Hawes would probably discover very few familiar to them.

We have no late publication strictly in our dialect, as the Barnsley and Leeds folk have in theirs. Some centuries ago the speech of this district appears to have been written as ordinary English of the time. Several of the Towneley (or Wakefield) Mysteries ['T.M.' in these notes] contain words and phrases which the characters in the plays must have uttered as purely Wakefield people of our time would speak them. Cayn, for instance, in the "Mactatio Abel," talks and swears like a fractious, Wakefield, blackguard of twenty years ago. Some of the words referred to will be found in the List. The following, from various plays, are clearly Wakefieldisms –

That *at* is dry......page	2	*ryfe* my hose	11
Both hold and drive ...	11	*were* my shoyn	11
a craw to pulle	15	*bi* this thyng be broght	
Sam together	27	to end	38
Is all for*geyn*?	42	toche now thi *thee*	
thou shalt not *swere* ...	50	[thigh]..................	47
Nere hand	98	fou*rt* commaundement	50
Adyld his ded	195	settes not a *fle* wyng *bi*	
Clowt his kap............	199	Sir Cesar	192
Be not to *breme*	197	go his gate	247
Open youre *yate*.........	248	*melle* the not with us...	248
roten inwardly as the *colke* within				281.

The ordinary method of representing dialect words, though not precise, is generally best understood; and, therefore, is employed here. Mr. W. L. Robinson's plan has the advantage of being both certain and simple to those who are acquainted with it; but unfortunately few are so, and for this reason an intention to print the words with his characters has been reluctantly given up.

W.S.B.

Wakefield, August, 1865

A Walk in the Country

THE SAMI OF LAPLAND have hundreds of words for different types of snow so it's not surprising to learn that walkers around Wakefield had half a dozen words for mud.

CLAGGY, sticky. "Claggy under fooit" means the mud sticks to the feet in walking.

SLAPPY, sloppy; wet underfoot.

SLUSHY, puddly.

SLUDGE, wet mud.

MUCK, manure or dirt. Mucky, dirty.

RAMLIN, perambulating. "Ramlin t' bahnderies."

CAUSEH, causeway, a flag'd footpath. FLEGS, the flag'd footpath. "Walk up o' t' flegs" "All t' rooads abaht here is fleg'd."

KNOWL, an elevation. "T' knowl o' t' hill."

SHENKS' MARE. To ride up o' "Shenks' mare" is to go on foot.

STAUPIN, long-striding. "Shoo's a greeat awkerd staupin' thing."

TRAPESIN, walking or draggling about in dirty weather. The use of the word implies censure.

TRESHIN, similar to trapesin.

Weather

Storm, rain and wind feature in these local words for weather but fine, sunny days don't get a mention. Middle English words like 'brim' and 'melch' are rarely used today.

MIZZLE, small rain.

WETS, rains slightly. "It raather wets a bit, bud it weeant be much."

TEEM, pour. "Teem it aht." "It teems dahn wi raan."

BRIM, sharp and keen. "T'wind's varry brim up o' t' *h*ill." In Chaucer it means sharp and furious. In Spenser, *Shepheardes Calender, February* we have:

"Eft when ye count you freed from fear,
Comes the *breme* winter with chamfred brows."

And see "brymly" T. M. 305.

The Shepheardes Calender, 1597

BLUSTERY, a wind coming in gusts, or blowing strongly.

EDGE O' DARK, and **COMIN DAY LEET**, express the close and dawn of day.

16

LEETNIN, lightning.

THUNNER, thunder.

MELCH, mild.
Applied to the
weather, it means
mild and moist.

RAW. We say of the
weather, "It's cowd
and raw."

RIME, hoar frost.

Birds

In May, 1865, the year that Banks compiled his list, pioneer conservationist Charles Waterton died, aged 83. His bird reserve at Walton Park soon came under threat.

DICKEY DUNNOK, the hedge sparrow.

DIVLIN. 1. A small cone of gunpowder, which, being worked up wet, does not explode, but "fizzes" slowly when lighted. 2. The swift.

FEATHERPOKE, nest of the long tailed Tit. Also the bird itself.

FLACKER, flutter, as with wings.

FLIG'D, fledged, feathered. "T' birds is full flig'd."

GEZLIN, gooseling, young goose; "a cletch o' gezlins."

GRASS DRAKE, corn crake, or landrail.

19

NANPIE, Magpie

NEB, a beak, as a bird's neb or bill; a cap neb; also the nose. "*He*'s allus stickin' *h*is neb into sum'dy's pint."

NEP, peck. "T' young birds can't nep yit"

PEWIT, the plover.

SHEP, a starling.

SPINK, a finch. Bull spink is bullfinch; gold spink, goldfinch.

STORMCOCK, the missel thrush.

THROS'LE, the song thrush.

ULLOT, an owl.

YOWLRING, the yellow-hammer.

Animals & Insects

Until 1820 the church wardens of Wakefield made payments for the destruction of 'vermin'. They paid tuppence for a mole or hedgehog and a shilling for an otter.

ARRANS, spiders.

COCK WEB, cobweb.

ASKERD, lizard. "Dry askerd," a land lizard. "Watter askerd," a newt.

BLACK CLOCKS, blackbeetles. "There's noa end o' black clocks i' t' *h*oil."

BROCK, the cuckoo-spit insect. "Sweeat like a brock."

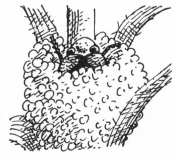

CUSHY CAH LAADY, the little beetle, *Coccinella septempunctata*.

ELSIN, an awl. "Elsin grooin"(or awl nose) was formerly used as a name for the mosquito.

FLEE, a fly.

MIDGE, a gnat.

FOOMAD, foumart, a pole cat. [The churchwardens paid fourpence for a foumart].

HORSE-TENGS, dragon flies, so called from a belief that they sting horses.

KINNLE, the bringing forth young by rabbits.

KITLIN, a kitten.

KITTLE, 1. bring forth kittens. 2. tickle. "Kittle as a mahstrap."

Lops, fleas. "Full o' *lops* an' lice."

Mahstrap, Mousetrap.

Mauks, maggots.

Milt, the spleen; also the male herring.
Roan, the roe of the female herring; also, that fish itself.

MOULDEWARP, the mole.

PISMIRES, ants.

PUP, the bringing forth young by dogs.

RATTEN, a rat.

SEG, Swollen-bellied rabbits are said to be segged when suffering from tubercular peritonitis.

SKUT, tail of hare or rabbit.

SNICKLE, a snare. A rabbit or hare snickle is a band or wire with a slipping loop.

TOMMY BARSE, the spiny backed fish, Ruffe, *Acerina vulgaris*.

TOM PAINER, a common yellowish beetle-like insect found on hawthorn. [probably the Hawthorn Shieldbug, *Acanthosoma haemorrhoidale*, a 'stink bug' which exudes a pungent fluid when alarmed.]

TWINGE, an earwig, *Forficula auricularia*.

UMMLEBEE or UMMABEE, the humble bee.

Plants

My father-in-law, William Ellis, who was born and brought up in post-World War I Wakefield, used the words 'wicks' *(p.48)* and 'dockins' when he helped me with weeding.

ACKERONS, acorns.

BLEGS, blackberries, bramble berries.

BRAMMLE, a bramble.

BULLACES, wild plums, sold often as damsons, but inferior. COBBLER BALLS, large, black, bitter plums.

CAT NUT, the earth nut, *Bunium flexuosum*. [now known as Pig-Nut, *Conopodium majus*].

CLEATS, the colt's foot or "foil foot." People get the flowers to make colt's-foot wine.

DEE NETTLES, nettles which do not sting, chiefly the *Lamium album* and *L. Purpureum*. "They weeant nettle cos they're nobbut dee nettles."

DOCKIN, usually the common broad leaved dock, *Rumex obtusifolius*.

Fuz Ball, the fungus *Lycoperdon gemmatum* [Common Puffball, now *Lycoperdon perlatum*].

GodMeit, young leaves of the hawthorn, which children eat in spring.

Green Sauce, common sorrel; *Rumex acetosa.*

Ketlock, *Sinapis arvensis.* Dr. Prior says it is the Anglo Saxon cedeleac—*leac*, a plant, and *cede,* which is perhaps related to the Danish *kiede,* to annoy.

KEX, the hogweed, *(Heracleum sphondylium)*, and other umbelliferous plants, such as cow-parsley.

SWADS, pods, as "pey swads."

WATTER BLOB, water lily; also the flower of the *Caltha palustris* [Marsh Marigold or Kingcups].

WITHIES, withes, willow sticks. "As tough as a withy."

BRACKENS, ferns with pinnate fronds.

CRESH, cress. As "watter cresh."

DAFFY DAHN DILLY, daffodil.

DOG DAASY, the common daisy.

ESH TREE, ash tree.

ESPIN, aspin. "It tremmles like a espin leeaf."

FAT *h*EN, the common weed, narrow leaved *orache* [*Chenopodium album*].

FETHERFAHL, the plant feverfew *Pyrethrum parthenium* [*Chrysanthemum parthenium*].

FITCHES, vetches.

HAAGS, haws, fruit of hawthorn.

GRUNSIL, groundsel; *Senecio vulgaris.*

HELLIN, an Elder tree.

*H*EP, hip, fruit of wild rose.

HOLLIN, the *H*olly tree.

I'VIN, ivy. "T'ivin weeant mak t' *h*ahse damp if yeh nobbud cut it cloisish to t'wall."

JILLIVER, the wallflower.

LAADY FING'R, the Laburnum flower.

NOP, a knob, a flower-bud. "T' roases is i' nop."

PISSIBED, the dandelion.

UMLOCK, hemlock. Applied to several umbelliferous plants.

WHINS, gorse or furze.

WIGGIN, mountain-ash tree.

WIZES, stalks of plants, as "tatey wizes."

YARBS, herbs.

Farming

In 1865 Wakefield had a weekly cattle market. The New Corn Exchange, which stood at the top of Westgate, on the right, was opened in 1838 and enlarged in 1864.

HOD OR DRIVE, a ploughman's phrase from times when the horses worked in single file. "Ah can't boath *hod* an drive," *i.e.*, hold the plough and drive the cattle. Cayn in Mac: Abel says, "Shall I bothe hald and drife?" T. M. 9. Also, "Com nar, and other drife or hald."—*Id*. The well-known proverb refers to this—

> "He that by the plough would thrive,
> Himself must either hold or drive."

One man does both now, each horse being harnessed to the plough.

Farming Fairs & Feast Days

PLOO STOTS [stot: a staggering, clumsy person], plough stots, farm servants, having patched dresses, and ribbon ends on hats and clothes, and blowing cows' horns, going round begging on Plough Monday [the first after Twelfth Night], with a plough-frame steered by the last married man, the two youngest lads being drivers, two of the eldest men the beggars, and the rest taking place of horses. The practice is almost gone out now, though one party, *without plough,* came into Wakefield in 1865, but on the *wrong* Monday—namely, a week too soon.

FORTNIT FAAR, the cattle fair in the fair ground begun here 27th March, 1765. On 23rd June, 1858, a weekly fair was commenced and it is very successful.

STATTIS, statute fair. "*H*ired at Waakfild stattis."

GODSPENNY, good penny (?); hiring money given yearly to farm servants.

LAHNCE, allowance; gift above wages, usually some beer to drink for an odd job, or as an extra. "Ye mun stand a drop o' lahnce."

PIND, impound. WAVER, the place where the pinfold and "Springs" are. Is Waver, *waifer*, the pound for estrays and waifs?

 LAATHE, a barn.

*H*AAH moo, a hay chamber.

*H*ELM, a shed for cattle in a field.

MISTLE, a cowhouse.

MIDDIN, a heap, as, "a muck middin;" or, "a ass (ash) middin."

*H*ECK, 1. hayrack. 2. a small gate. "Shut t' *h*eck after theh."

DYKE, a ditch.

YATE, gate.

SWARTH, sward. "A nice swarth up o' that grass plat."
PLAT, plot, as "grass-plat."

FOG, aftergrass. [growth after the first crop has been mown. Yorkshire Fog, *Holcus lanatus* is also known as Velvet Grass because of the soft hairs on its stems and leaves].

39

KIVVER, a set of corn sheaves built up in the field to dry.

RIG, ridge, back. "Ah'll tak it o' my rig;" "there's a lot o'sparrahs up o't'*h*ahse rig."

*H*OPPIT, a small round basket. A straw bee-hive is a "bee hoppit;"

EKE, an increase or addition, as an eke (a bottom rim) to a bee hive.

IMP, an eke, or addition, to a straw bee hoppit; "put a imp on it."

TENT, 1. prevent. "Ah'l tent theh." To tent birds is to frighten them from newly sown or ripening corn.

2. watch or take care of, as tent cattle when feeding in lanes. An engine fireman is an engine tenter.

FAAH IN. To "faah t' muck in," is to spread dung dropt in a field by cattle.

FAUF, fallow. "By t' look o' yer booits ye've been in a fauf cloise."

STOVVEN, a stem; also, a stump. A hedge cut down "to t' stovvens" is cut so as to leave only the stumps of the shrubs.

RADDLE, to interlace or intwine. "We just raddled a faew sticks into t' fence to keep t' beeas aht."

STUB, dig up. To stub a fence is to dig out the roots. See *Northern Farmer* [dialect poem by Tennyson].

STOOP, a post set in the ground. We call a post and rail fence "stoops an raals."

HOG, a male pig.

SAH, a sow.

GILT, a young female pig before it attains the matronly name of "sow;" "oppen gilt" is unspayed sow.

GRECK, the wreckling or weakling, as of a litter of pigs, the least.

GROOIN, pigs snout; "two swyne gronys," T. M. 89.

SKUTTERIN, running hurriedly. "T' litter or pigs cam skutterin aht o' t' coit."

MUCKT AHT, cleaned out. "T' pig-coit wants muckin aht."

TUP, 1, a ram. 2, run at and strike with the head.

KIT, a milk-pail, or other wooden pail.

BEEAS, beasts, horned cattle.

BEEST, a cow's first milk after calving.

NOIT, the period of milk-giving. Cows are "fresh noited," or "*ow*d noited."

FELLON'D, hidebound. "t' cah's fellon'd; *h*er *h*ide' sas fast as *ow*t." [hidebound; having dry skin closely attached to the underlying flesh because of poor feeding].

HOBBLE. "In a *hobble*" is in a difficulty or perplexity; hobbled, as cattle are when the legs are tied together, or a log is tied to one leg.

FOTHER, feed cattle in doors. "Fother up," is bed and feed for the night.

NOITER, neat-herd, herdsman of neats— Anglo Saxon for cattle.

RED RUDDLE, such as is used for marking cattle.

CLETCH, a brood, as a cletch of chickens. "A bonny (large) cletch o' barns."

CHUCK, 1. throw a short way. "Chuck t' ball ovver *h*eeare."2. Name for barn door hen; and the word used in calling poultry. 3. choke, as "chuck up"or "chuck full"—choke full.

SITTIN, hatching. "T' *ow*d un's *h*ard an fast a sittin."
CLOCK, the cluck of a hen. "A clockin *h*en," is a hen wanting to "sit."

LARP or LAHK, pull weeds out of corn by hand. "Larpin' ketlocks."

SPITTLE, a little spade (?). We do call a spade a spade; but this word is used here, as elsewhere, in baking-spittle. In digging, also, we speak of a spade-breadth as a "spittle-breadth;" and shaving off weeds from the surface of the ground with a spade we call "spittlin' weeds."

WICK, 1. to wick, is to pull up wick, or quick, grass.
2. quick, alive. "Ah doant knaw what it is, bud it's summat at's wick."
WICKS, quicks; several species of agrosta, of which *Agrostis vulgaris* is considered the worst as a weed in arable land.

[Common Bent grass or Browntop (now known as *Agrostis tenuis*) makes poor grazing but is used in fine lawns and bowling greens.]

The Horse Trade

If you needed to get somewhere, your choice
was either to use horse power or to walk. In
1865, transport using fossil fuels was limited
to the railways and to steam traction engines.

COCKELTY, not firmly
rested. "T' stee's
raather cockelty and
if teh doesn't mind
it'll tummle wi theh."

FELK, a felloe for a
wheel. [A felloe is a
segment of the rim of
a wooden wheel].

NAFF, the nave of a
carriage wheel.

GEE. This and other calls used in driving horses are, I suppose, common to many parts of the kingdom. *Gee*, is go on

Cum hether, come hither [the hitherside is the nearside, *i.e.* left].

Cum up, start or go faster

Whet gee, away go, *i.e.*, turn to off side [right].

Whoi-e, who-o-ie, or *whei*, stop.

Joss, jolt. "T'rooad wor full o' ruts, an - we wor varry neear jost aht o' t' cart."

SLAPE SHOD, shod in a slippery way. "T' horse is so slape shod, he can't hod his sen dahn hill,"

SLUFF, slough. "Heart sluft" is heartbroken. A horse dying from over-driving is said to be "heart sluft."

SPRAG, a stout club used for pushing between the spokes of tram waggon wheels to stop them.

ARRIDGE, a ridge or edge. A "sharp arridge" on a horse shoe is the projection in front to enable the horse to keep on his feet when drawing.

BUR, stop. "Bur t' wheel wi a stone."

FETTLE, condition or state as, "t' horse wor e good fettle." Also to clean or make trim.

MUELE, mule, an ass.

RAWM, to rear, as, "a rawmin horse," or, "a rawmin lion."

REESTY, 1. rusty (?), as "reesty" (or rancid) bacon. 2. restive, as a "reesty" horse.

SHOG, slow trot. "Went shoggin on."

STITHY, an anvil.

STY. Sty is explained to mean narrow road, Anglo Saxon *Stya*. A bridle sty road is a road for horses only (not carriages). See T. M. 16. and Glossary.

TIT, a horse. "Good sort on a tit that."

WHIPPIN O'GALLEWEHS, hasty running or driving about.

Water

A watermill, the King's Mill, stood by the Chantry Chapel bridge, near the head-quarters and warehouses of the the Aire and Calder Navigation Company. The navigation had been established by Act of Parliament in 1698 and Wakefield became a busy inland port. In 1840, the Canal Company attempted to stop George Stephenson's plans to bring the Lancashire and Yorkshire Railway through the town, crossing Kirkgate.

BAADE, bathe.

BAAL-AHT, to "lade" out, as getting water out of boats with a small water bucket.

BECK, a small stream, as "Ings beck," a name common over the N.W. and N.E. of Yorkshire.

COCK BOAT, a small boat, such as may be propelled by sculling or with a pair of oars.

DOWSE, throw water upon. "Gie it a good dowsin." Sound *ow* as in cow.

DRAANDIN, drowning. "It gat draanded."

LAADIN CAN, a small "can" (tin vessel) used for lading, or removing, liquids out of a larger holder.

MILL RACE, mill stream.

PIGGIN, a small pail with one stave left long for a handle, used as a "lading" vessel.

SIPE, to draw through or out of "T' watter *he*s all sided through t' eearth." "Let t' bottle sipe aht."

55

SLAHT, sprinkle or splash. "Shoo dipt t' brush into t'gutter *h*oil an slahted *h*im all ower wi mucky watter."

STAITH or STAAH, a place by the river for shipping goods. "Coil staah."

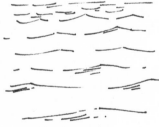

WATTER, water.

W*ei*KEY, damp; soaked with wet.

Food

With the exception of treacle, sugar, ginger, rice and currants, all the foods mentioned here could be locally grown or reared. Also included; words used in the butcher's trade.

AVVER BREEAD, oaten bread.

BAAKIN SPITTLE. Spittle, a spade (little spade ?) Flat wooden spade to turn cakes with when baking.

BACKSTON, baking stone.

BADGER, meal-seller. To "badger" is also to banter in price; also to teaze.

BAESTIN T' M*eit*, is pouring fat over the meat as it roasts.

BLATTER, batter. "Blatter puddin'."

BRANDREY, an iron frame to hold Yorkshire pudding when baking before the fire under meat. [Were brandy snaps originally "brandrey snaps"; a sweet batter baked in a brandrey?]

CAHCUMMER, cucumber.

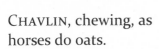

CAMMERIL, a notcht stick used by butchers to hang up a carcase by pushing it through the ham strings.

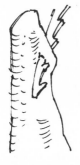

CHAVLIN, chewing, as horses do oats.

CRACKLIN CAKE, thin and crisp wheaten cake.

COLLOP MONDAY, day before Shrove
Tuesday. Children had a custom, and in
some places have yet, of giving their School
teacher bacon collops and eggs on this day.
People thought no luck would attend them
all the year if they did not dine on bacon
collops this day.

*"Collop Monday; pancake Tuesday; fruttis
Wednesday, an hey for Thursday afternooin."*

COLLOPS, slices of
bacon, "bacon
collops." I have not
heard it applied to
any other food.

FRUTTIS, a fritter.
"Fruttis Wedensdeh,"
is Ash Wednesday.
AFTERNOOININ,
refreshment between
dinner and tea.

CURNS, currants.
Curnberries, currant
berries.

DAAZ'D, dull and
pale. Animal food or
bread not browned
in cooking is "nasty
daaz'd stuff not fit
to *eit*."

DRIDGIN BOX, a flour
box with holes in the
top used for
dredging, or
sprinkling, flour upon
pastry or other food.

EGG CRATCH, a frame
with holes for
holding eggs.

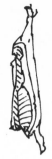

FLICK, a flitch. [side of meat, usually bacon]

FRUMMATY, furmity [frumenty]. Creed wheat boil'd in milk, usually done at Christmas. Corn-factors and millers generously supply their friends with a small bag of wheat at that time.

HAASTY-PUDDIN, flour of wheat or oats boiled in water or milk, poured on a plate and eaten with treacle, or into a basin of milk.

HAVVER, oat. "Havver caak" is oaten cake. "Havver janok" is a name for dry oat cake. It appears by documents of title that near the Shutts were lands called the "havver lands."

LAMB PURTENCE, a
lamb's head, with its
appurtenances, heart,
lungs, and liver.
PLUCK, the lungs,
heart, and liver of a
sheep or calf.

LITHENIN,
thickening, as of
broth or milk with
flour; or to stiffen, as
"lithe his ribs wi
haasty puddin."

LOBSCOUSE, animal
food, potatoes, and
onion; stew'd
together in the oven.
Irish stew.

LOWSNIN SUPPER, a
supper given when a
youth is "loose" from
his apprenticeship.
Sometimes rearing sup-
pers are given by build-
ers when a building has
been rear'd or built up.

MINCH, mince, as, "minch pies."

MUNGE, munch. "*E*it thy m*e*it r*e*it; doan't munge it i that waah."

MURPHIES, potatoes. TATEYS, potatoes. PILLINS, peelings, as "tatey pillins," for potato peelings.

MUSHERAM, mushroom. "Musheram catchup." [A rich, pungent condiment used with meat and game and in pies, puddings and soups.]

PANSHON, an earthenware bowl for domestic purposes.

PARKIN, bread consisting of oatmeal and treacle, customarily made for the 5th of November; called also "treacle parkin."

POSNIT, an iron pan for boiling liquids, having either a hooped or a side handle.

REKON, a movable iron bar with pendant crook, and holes to regulate the height, used for hanging pans over a fire.

ROWLY POWLY
PUDDIN, a pudding
made of fruit and a
thin cake of dough,
rolled and boiled.

SALLIT, salad;
usually and strictly,
lettuce only.

SAME, pigs lard. "A
blether o' same" is a
bladder of lard. [Pig's
bladders were used
in the manufacture
of footballs and
rugby balls.]

SCOREIN, drawing
lines across, as
cutting the skin of
pork before cooking.

SILE, to strain. A milk
sile is a strainer.

SNAP, or BRANDY
SNAP, thin ginger-
bread sold at fairs.

SPICE, sweet
things for sucking,
made chiefly of
sugar, or treacle.

STORKEN, stiffen, as
mutton gravy does.

BLETHER, a bladder.

BUTTER SCOTCH, butter and sugar boiled together, say one weight of butter to two of sugar.

CAN, a tin vessel for carrying liquids; usually "tin can."

CARCASS, body of beast or human being dead or alive. "Blaame his carcass."

CLAMM'D, pined for want of food. "Clamm'd to deeath."

CRAPS, the skin remaining after "rendering" fat, as, "talleh craps," or "pig craps." [Pork scratchings]

CRATCH, a butcher's frame to kill pig or sheep on.

CREE, soften with liquid. Rice is creed, or steept, in heated milk or water for puddings; wheat for furmity.

DOAF, dough.

EIT, eat.

ETTEN, eaten. "Come as sooin as thah's etten thy dinner." "Ah'll come nah for ah can *ei*t nowt."

KELL, the omentum [membrane covering and supporting internal organs such as the stomach and liver].

KET, carrion, animal flesh unfit for food of man.

LEETS, 1. lungs. 2. lights.

MANNIFOLD, the third stomach of the ox.

MESH'L'TUN, mixture of rye flour and wheat flour.

MIDGRAM, mesentery [tissue that holds organs to the body wall]. Commonly that of the pig is meant.

Pax Wax, the neck tendon seen in "cuts" of beef "As tough as pax wax."

Porridge, milk boiled and lithened (thickened) with flour.

Puddins, intestines.

Render, melt animal fat, as inside fat of pigs for lard.

Rops, the small intestines of animals.

Sharps, the skin drest off wheat by millers after the removal of the bran.

Shivs, or Shivvins, husks taken off grain, as off oats.

Slafterhahse, slaughter-bouse.

Slaps, slops.

Swillins, kitchen refuse for pig-food.

Childhood and Schooldays

In 1865 the town had a 'Churchey Schooil' and a 'Lanky (Lancastrian) Schooil', both dating from 1813. The Old Grammar School (1591) was then a Green-Coat School for 'poor boys'.

BARNS, children. "A byrd hav I broght to my barne." T. M. i 18. "A madyn a barn shuld here." T. M. 158

DILLY *h*OIL, OR *h*AHSE, a little house, or place, for children to play in.

MADDL'D, confounded, perplexed. "Ahm, ommost maddl'd wi t' din at ye barns is makkin."

MAWNGEY, mangey, as a petted and spoiled child. "Thah'rt a little mawngey tooad."

PIN A SEET, a child's show, a pin a sight.

SKOPPERIL, a toy made with a pin through a button, or small round plate, for spinning.

THRIP BOX, a thrift box; a box for a child's savings.

A-B-C's, the common English alphabet. "Can *he* sa-ah *h*is A-B-C's ?"

ANPARCY, the &c. Children in "saying" their alphabet used to run on, "—x.y.z, anparcy."

BRAT, a child's pinafore; also the child itself.

CHILDER, children.

CHONCE BARN, an illegitimate child. "Shoo *h*ed *h*im by chonce."

DOY, joy, a loving name for a child. "Bless theh doy. "

LAD, boy; familiarly used to men also.

> "*Judas.* Good sir, take it no grefe.
> "*Anna.* We, lad, thou shuld ask lefe."

> T. M. 176.

LAHRN, learn, to teach. "Whose lahrn'd theh thee letters?"

LEAD-EATER, India-rubber used for rubbing pencil marks out of paper.

SAID, quieted, or obedient. "They're t'warst barns is ars at ivver wor; they weeant be said at no*w*t." "*H*e's said wi' a word."

SLIP, a child's pinafore.

T*ei*CH, teach.

TING-A-LING, a child's imitation of a bell.

UP A DAASY, a nurse's phrase when dancing a child in her hands.

Supernatural Tales

In *Wakefield, its History and its People*, J. W. Walker tells us that, from as long ago as 1766, a well-known Padfoot haunted Westgate; it was the size of a calf, with a shaggy coat, glowing saucer-sized eyes and twisted horns.

The Boggard of Langar hede, another Padfoot, could seen walking beside the wall of Alverthorpe Hall. It had a white furry coat and, like the Westgate Padfoot, dragged a clanking iron chain behind it.

PAD FOOIT, a supposed supernatural being on four feet "wi greeat saucer een," waylaying people in lonely places, spoken of as "t' pad fooit." Is this an inversion of Footpad, a highway robber?

BARGEST, an apparition. What sort of ghost? The word is used also as a term of abuse.

BOGGARD, a ghost or apparition. "T' black boggard" is spoken of as if one personage or thing.

Owd LAD, the devil; also a friendly name. "That's r*eight*, *owd* lad."

SCRAT, 1, "*owd* Scrat," or "*owd* Scratch," is the devil. 2. to scratch.

All Kinds of Talk

No phrase book would be complete without some everyday greetings. While 'Hah goes it?' and 'Owt fresh?' would be understood in 21st century Wakefield, we wouldn't recommend 'Hey, missus, come heear.'

Hah Goes It? a salutation.

  Owt Fresh? a salutation. Common answer, "Naah, nowt; what's t' best news wi' thee?"

Hey! a call to attract attention. "Hey, missis, come heear." Sometimes, "hey up."

WHAT CHEER! a salutation.

MIDDLIN, tolerably well. "*H*ah ar yeh ?" "'Middlin, thenk yeh."

AAH-BA, a loud vulgar laugh or shout. "What ar teh makkin that gert *Aah -ba* for?"

CALLIN, calling. Used deprecatingly of the practice of women wasting their time gossiping with neighbors.

CAMPIN, similar to callin; but usually meaning to stand gossiping in street or yard. "Shoo stans campin at t' yard end thrugh morn to neet."

DRAAT, drawl. "Ah *h*aate to *h*ear onybody draate when theh read."

MAUNDER, talk incoherently, or in a low tone grumblingly. "What are teh maundrin thear abaht?"

NOMMANY, a preamble, a formal saying or proclaiming. The crier at Quarter Sessions, on opening or adjourning the Court, uses "some mack on a nommany," beginning with "Oyez! oyez!"

PRATE, talk pertly or saucily, as in case of a young person to an elder. "Doan't stand pratin to me."

SNAVVEL, sniffle; talk or breathe noisily through the nose.

STEVVEN, the voice. "Thah's a rare stevven, lad."

"*Abelle.* God that Shope both erth and heven, I pray to thee that thou hear my steven."

T. M. 12.

"I hard by his steven He was sent down fro heven."   *Id.* 94.

ABAHT R*eigh*T, right, or rightly.

AYE, sounded I, yes. Our commonest affirmative. See "Ei" also.

CALL, 1. scold. 2 need for. "Thear worn't noa call for no*w*t o' t' soart."

CLACK, noisy talk. "Ahm tired o' thy clack."

CRACK, boast: "They crack rarely o' theh."

CUDDLE, to embrace the neck.

CURCHY, curtsey.

DIN, noise. "*H*od thy din."

DROP IT, be quiet. "Nah, drop it! what's teh' plaagin me for?"

EI, yes. "Wi teh goa?" "Ei in a minnit." See "aye" also.

GAB, speech. "Gift o' t'gab" is facility of speech.

*H*UM'D *A*N *h*AW'D, hesitated in speech.

PRETHEH, pray thee. "Pretheh *h*od thy noise; thah's said enif"

SAUCE, pert or forward talk. "Ah want noan o' thy sauce."

ST*ei*M, give an order.

STUTTS, stammers.

WHISHT! command to be silent.

YOWL, howl.

Weights & Measures

From 'time immemorial' the lords of the manor of Wakefield claimed the right to check the weights and measures of the district. In 1892 Wakefield clubbed together with other local authorities and the West Riding County Council to buy this right.

This 1 lb weight was kite-marked on 31 May 1855. It carries the 'MW' stamp of the manor of Wakefield.

WARTREN, a weight of six pounds. A term used in the blanket and yarn trades.

NUMBERS
TOANE, the one.
"Toane or tuther."
TOATHRE, two or three; a few.
BAAKER'S DOZEN, thirteen.

Quantities

SMALL CHANGE
TUP'NCE, twopence.
We say "thrip'nce,
fip'nce," and so on.

GOOD FAEW, good few, a good many.

FAEW, few. "A goodish faew" is a moderate number.

SKERRICK, a very small quantity. "Not a skerrick left."

LITTLE TINY, small. In T. M. 96. second Shepherd, addressing the babe Jesus, says:—"Haylle, lytylle tyne mop!"

ALL NOWT, nothing. "It's all nowt."

WAPPER, a great thing. "That's a wapper."

DOLLOP, a great quantity.

PART, a large quantity. "Thear's part ooats grown abaht."

GERT, GREEAT, GREEAT BIG, great.

AWFISH, halfish, neither well nor ill.

RAARELY, great, or much, or well. "They've gotten into a raare mess;" "-they've brokken, an ahm raarely in wi' 'em;" "*he's* raarely off sin' *h*e gat that brass."

Time

Banks compiled his list of Wakefield Words in August, 1865. On 30 August, the highly successful Wakefield Industrial and Fine Art Exhibition, which he had helped to promote, opened in the Tammy Hall and in a purpose-built hall on Wood Street.

In that year:

April 15: Abraham Lincoln was assassinated as the American Civil War drew to an end.

July 14: Edward Whymper climbed the Matterhorn.

October: end of transportation of criminals to Australia.

December 18: Slavery abolished in the USA.

Britain's population was 29 million, of which 60 per cent worked in industry.

CLICK, catch at; also a sharp sound, as the ticking of a clock.

QUARTER JACKS, the quarter-hour strokes of the public clock.

SATTLIN T' BELLS, lowering a peel of bells after a full ringing. "It's church time; they're sattlin t' bells."

TIC TAC, the beat of clock or watch; a short space of time. "Be back in a tic tac."

T' OTHER DAAH, a day or two since, an unascertained day not long past. "It wor nobbut t' other daah at it *h*appened."

Proverbs

The maxims and sayings of the district are not remarkable for poetic expression, or tenderness even, or, indeed, anything better than the most ordinary "worldly wisdom." They are nearly all of the earth, earthy, and denote no more originality or sense in the user than the commonest verb in the vocabulary; but they are always accepted as wise and indisputable. The following are some of these :—

A daay after t' fair.

Aht on *his* *h*eead.

As short as Dick's hatb'nd at went nine times rahand an' wodn't tee.

The 'Dick' here is fun-loving Richard Cromwell (1626-1712), son of Oliver, whose brief stint wearing the 'crown' of Lord Protector ended with his abdication in May 1659.

Doant buy a pig in a poak.

A poke is a bag or small sack. The saying refers to the trick, when selling a suckling pig at market, of palming off the unwary buyer with a cat. Opening the poke was 'Letting the cat out of the bag'.

As big as bull beef.

As deead as a doar naal.

As deeaf as a doar naal.

As *h*appy as pigs e muck.

Cuttin' off yer noase to spite yer faace.

Cut yer coit accordin' to yer cloth.

Doant kick a chap when *h*e's dahn.

Doant reckon yer chickins afore ther *h*etcht.

Do fair.

Done up stump an rump.

Drop it an call it *h*auf a daah.

Follerin' yer noase.

Hobson's choice, that or noan.

Thomas Hobson (*c.* 1544-1631), the Cambridge carrier, insisted on letting out his horses in strict rotation and wouldn't let his customers choose among them.

Girn an' bide it.

*H*evin yer noase up o' t' grinleston.

If foaks does *owt* at's wreng its suer to come *h*oame by 'em.

If t' sky wor to tum'le ye'd catch larks.

In for a penny in for a pahnd.

It's a ill wind at blows noabody good.

Led by t'noase.

Mad as a March *h*aare.

Mak a dash on it.

Payin' thrugh t' noase.

Penny wise and pahnd fooilish.

Puttin' *h*is noase aht o' joint.

Saddle *h*im wi' it.

Saafe as a thief in a mill.

Shut t' stable doar when t' *h*orse is stown.

Sue a beggar and get a lahse.

Talk o' t' divvel and *h*e'll awther come er rattle *h*is cheins.

To get seckt.

To much on a good thing's good for nowt.

T' tune at t'*ow*d cah deed on.

Tuk it up on *h*is awn *h*eead.

Two blacks doant mak a white.

Warse things is an better, 'cos they're suer to mend sooin.

What's bred i' t' boan ah'll nivver get aht o' t' flesh.

What's gotten ovver t' divvle's back 'll be spent under *h*is belly.

There are many more [like sayings] in use among us. It will be seen that most of them are common to many parts of England.

Pronunciation

Banks included these notes on pronouns, pronunciation, and vocal contractions.

The Wakefield dialect has at least two sounds which appear shut out from national English speech, and competent men think rightly. These are *ow* and *eigh*, or *ei*, as in grow and neigh, which we are told to utter like *o* in so and *a* in lay, thus making bow into *boe*, row into *roe*, weight into *wate*, and eight into *ate*. People who know the dialects of this and neighboring towns, will not require any explanation of these sounds. It is hoped that those who do not will be able to learn them thus—the vowels in *now* and *cow* may be represented by *ah-oo*. Substitute the *aw* of *law* for *ah*, and pronounce the diptbong *aw-oo* as rapidly as the *ah-oo* of cow is sounded, and that will be nearly right. The sound *eigh* is got at by a quick utterance of *a* as in *late* and *i* as in *sit*—*a-i*. The *ow* and *eigh*, or *ei*, when sounded in this manner are printed in italic. Aspirates are seldom, if ever, used in the dialect; and though *H* is employed in the book for the purpose of shewing what the words are, the sign is printed in italic to mark its silence. Such words as *who* and *whose* are not marked, but they, also, are not aspirated. As mentioned in the list, the indefinite article *an* is seldom used; but *a* only. The *j* sound of g, also, is shewn by italics. *Eh*, which is often used, is intended to represent the sound of *e* in serv'd, for which we have no proper sign.

A pronounced *A-ah,* A; an. The article *an* is seldom used in the dialect. We say "a ahnce" (an ounce); "a egg;" "a owd *h*eead". We do say "a nuther;" "a nod glass;" and "a nod un."

A. E. I. O. U. Y. The vowel sounds used in this district do not differ *systematically* from those of common English. The speech is not a mere vulgarism; and, so far as I can see, no *rule* can be constructed on the subject of the differences. Where, for instance, the *a* as sounded in *bat* would be employed in the national speech, we, in some words, use the *e* of send, as in *benkt* and *shenks;* but we say *band, sand, hat, hand.* In like manner we sometimes sound the *a* of far correctly, or at most a little broadly, as in *barley;* sometimes differently, as in *fath'r* and *fa-a'ther.* Where *ea* would be the vowel we have *eigh* (or *ei)* or *ee-a,* or the *a* of *sat.* Thus—*meil, steil, speik,* for meal, steal, speak; *see-al, pee-al, bree-ach,* for seal, peal, breach. Reach is *reich* or *rack,* as *reich it heear; rack o' my ee.* In case of the *i* of pine, we use *finn'd* for find, but we also say *thine* and *mine.* The *ou* of bound is represented by *ah* or *u, bahnd* or *bun;* found is *fun.* The *oo* of such words as moon and soon is often pronounced *oo-i,* as *moo-in, soo-in;* but we say *book, look, groom, smook* [old spelling of *smoke*?], while *tuck* stands for took.

The *a* of b*a*te is usually lengthened into the dipthong *a-e (e* as in s*e*rv'd). I have represented this by *a-a.* The *a* of call, and, indeed, a majority of the vowels are commonly drawn out in a similar manner, as *caw-el* for call; *lee-an* for lean; *i-eron* for iron; *go-an* for gone; *bo-at* for boat; *ew-se* for use. And there is a broadening of the *a* of bat, *e* of pet, *i* of pit, *i* of bird, *o* of pot, *oo* of good, *oi* of boil, *ew* of new, and *u* of but.

Aн, I. "Ah weeant," I won't. See "I," and "Meh."

Eн. This sign, used often in the book, is to be

sounded like *e* in s*e*rv'd.

IT, 1. in the. "It cloise," is in the close. 2. its. "Let's gi theh a leg up on to it back." 3. meaning punishment, or other thing understood. "Thah'l catch it when teh gets *h*oam." "Neet after neet, and niver at *h*oam; ah can't stan it." "Ah sahnt goa"—"Wha, it's reight." "Shift thy sen; theear, that's it."

I, the personal pronoun, is sometimes sounded almost as in national English; sometimes as *ah*; sometimes as *i* in pit—"*I* sahnt," "*ah* weeant," "not if *I* knaw it." See under "Meh."

MEH, me. "Gi meh thy *h*and." When this pronoun is used emphatically it is pronounced *me*. "It's noan o' me." In like manner, as the sense requires, I is *i* (as in bit), or *ah*, or sometimes almost as in national English; we is *weh* or *we*; thou, *teh* or *thah*; thee, *theh* or *thee*; ye, *yeh* or *ye*; he, *ee* or *i* (as in b*i*t); she, *sheh* or *shoo*; our, *wer* or *ahr*, or *ehz*; your, *yer* or *yahr*; their, *ther* or *their*. Many other vocal contractions are made, as *wiv*, for we have; *witteh*, for wilt thou?

'S, the sign of the possessive case is not often used when the name of the thing possessed follows. We say, "a lad *h*at;" "a lass bonnit;" but when the name is understood, it is used, thus: "Whose is it?" "It's t' woman's."

SEN, self. Sens, selves, as "*h*issen," "*h*ersen," "thersens," "wersens," or "ehzsens."

TEH, thou. "Can teh read writin?" When emphatic, thou is "thah."

THAH, thou. See "Teh"and "Meh."

THEH, thee. "Ah'll sp*e*ik to theh in a minnit." See under "Meh."

THER, their. "It tuml'd up o' the' *h*eeads." When emphatic, we say *their*. See "Meh."

YE, you; used in the singular. "Ah dident!" Answer : "Ye did."

YEH, ye. "Ah sal tell o' yeh."

YER, your. "Give us yer *h*and, owd lad." See Yahr."

YAHR, the emphatic form of your. "It's yahrs." See "Yer"